First Facts™

Positively Pets

# Caring for Your
# Hermit Crab

by Adele Richardson

**Consultant:**
Jennifer Zablotny, DVM
Member, American Veterinary Medical Association

Capstone
press®

First Facts is published by Capstone Press,
151 Good Counsel Drive, P.O. Box 669, Mankato, Minnesota 56002.
www.capstonepress.com

*Library of Congress Cataloging-in-Publication Data*
Richardson, Adele, 1966–
    Caring for your hermit crab / [Adele Richardson].
    p. cm.—(First facts. Positively pets)
    Summary: "Describes caring for a hermit crab, including supplies needed, feeding, cleaning,
health, and safety"—Provided by publisher.
    Includes bibliographical references (p. 23) and index.
    ISBN-13: 978-0-7368-6388-9 (hardcover)
    ISBN-10: 0-7368-6388-5 (hardcover)
    1. Hermit crabs as pets—Juvenile literature.  I. Title. II. Series.
SF459.H47R53 2007
639'.67—dc22                                                        2006006390

**Editorial Credits**
Mari Schuh, editor; Bobbi J. Wyss, designer; Kim Brown, illustrator; Kelly Garvin,
    photo researcher/photo editor

**Photo Credits**
Capstone Press/Karon Dubke, cover, 5, 7, 8, 13, 15, 16, 21
Dwight R. Kuhn, 6, 10–11, 14, 18–19
Minden Pictures/Tui De Roy, 20

Capstone Press thanks Pet Expo in Mankato, Minnesota, for assistance with photo shoots.

1 2 3 4 5 6 11 10 09 08 07 06

# Table of Contents

So You Want to Own a Hermit Crab?........................................... 4

Supplies to Buy ....................................................................... 6

Your Hermit Crab's Home ....................................................... 9

Feeding Your Hermit Crab...................................................... 10

Cleaning ................................................................................. 12

Is My Hermit Crab Sick? ........................................................ 14

Keeping Your Hermit Crab Safe.............................................. 17

Your Hermit Crab's Life .......................................................... 19


Wild Relatives!........................................................................ 20

Decode Your Hermit Crab's Behavior .................................... 21

Glossary.................................................................................. 22

Read More .............................................................................. 23

Internet Sites........................................................................... 23

Index....................................................................................... 24

# So You Want to Own a Hermit Crab?

Knock! Knock! A hermit crab taps on its **aquarium** at the pet store. It's trying to bury itself in the sand. You want a hermit crab. But are you ready for the **responsibility**?

Learn how to take care of a hermit crab before you buy one. These popular pets are easier to care for than most pets.

I like to be with other hermit crabs. Please bring two or three of us home.

5

# Supplies to Buy

Your hermit crab will need a home. Buy it an aquarium with a top. The bigger it is, the better. The aquarium should be at least 5 gallons (19 liters).

Your hermit crab will also need other supplies. Get sand, food, water, and bowls. Hermit crabs don't grow their own shells. So buy extra shells for them.

# Your Hermit Crab's Home

Hermit crabs like to **burrow** in sand. Put a few inches of damp sand on the aquarium bottom.

Move slowly until your crab gets used to you. Quietly set the food and water bowls in the aquarium. The bowls should be only 2 inches (5 centimeters) deep.

I like my tank to be between 75 and 85 degrees Fahrenheit (24 and 29 degrees Celsius). I don't feel good if I get too warm or too cold.

75°F-85°F

# Feeding Your Hermit Crab

Feed your hermit crab every evening. Hermit crabs are **nocturnal**, so they wake up at night. Buy hermit crab food at pet stores. Hermit crabs can also eat fresh fruits and vegetables.

Just like you, I need calcium to stay healthy. You can help me get more calcium by feeding me cuttlebone, the inside shell of a cuttlefish.

11

# Cleaning

Cleaning up after hermit crabs doesn't take much time. Wash the food and water bowls every day. Get rid of uneaten food from the sand. Empty and clean the aquarium every few months. Then put in a few inches of fresh sand.

# Is My Hermit Crab Sick?

You may notice your hermit crab moving slowly and eating less. Maybe it buried itself. It's probably **molting**. Crabs shed their skin about once a year.

Make sure your pet has a dark area to molt. Put water nearby. Then leave it alone. If it stays buried more than four weeks, call a **veterinarian**.

# Keeping Your Hermit Crab Safe

You can safely play with your hermit crab outside of the aquarium. Put him on smooth floors so he won't snag a claw on the carpet. Keep other pets away.

Your hermit crab enjoys living with other hermit crabs. Just make sure you give them lots of shells. That way, they won't fight over them.

Pick me up from the back or top of my shell. Keep your hand flat when you hold me. Otherwise, I might get scared and pinch you.

# Your Hermit Crab's Life

Take good care of your hermit crab. Then it can live a long life. Most hermit crabs can live from 6 to 15 years. Being a good pet owner will keep your hermit crab healthy its whole life.

# Wild Relatives!

Your hermit crab has big relatives called coconut crabs. They can weigh up to 9 pounds (4 kilograms). They earned their name because they can crack open coconuts.

# Decode Your Hermit Crab's Behavior

- Hermit crabs like to live in groups. Sometimes a hermit crab will rub its antennas against another hermit crab to say "hi."

- Hermit crabs sometimes climb over each other or push each other around. Don't worry, this is normal. They are deciding who is in charge of the group.

- A scared or hurt hermit crab will look for a dark place to hide.

- Your hermit crab may hide in its shell when your shadow suddenly passes over it. It is just trying to protect itself. It will come back out when it feels safe again.

# Glossary

**aquarium** (uh-KWAIR-ee-uhm)—a glass tank where pets, including hermit crabs, hamsters, and fish, are kept

**burrow** (BUR-oh)—to dig a hole or tunnel

**molt** (MOHLT)—to shed old skin so new skin can grow

**nocturnal** (nok-TUR-nuhl)—active and awake at night

**responsibility** (ri-spon-suh-BIL-uh-tee)—a duty or a job

**veterinarian** (vet-ur-uh-NER-ee-uhn)—a doctor who treats sick or injured animals

# Read More

**Binns, Tristan Boyer.** *Hermit Crabs.* Keeping Unusual Pets. Chicago: Heinemann, 2004.

**Nelson, Robin.** *Pet Hermit Crab.* First Step Nonfiction. Minneapolis: Lerner, 2003.

**Schaefer, Lola.** *Hermit Crabs.* Musty-Crusty Animals. Chicago: Heinemann, 2002.

# Internet Sites

FactHound offers a safe, fun way to find Internet sites related to this book. All of the sites on FactHound have been researched by our staff.

Here's how:

1. Visit *www.facthound.com*

2. Choose your grade level.

3. Type in this book ID **0736863885** for age-appropriate sites. You may also browse subjects by clicking on letters, or by clicking on pictures and words.

4. Click on the **Fetch It** button.

**FactHound will fetch the best sites for you!**

# Index

behavior, 4, 9, 10, 14, 15,
    17, 21

cleaning, 12
cuttlebone, 10

feeding, 10

molting, 14–15

playing, 17

relatives, 20

sickness, 14–15
sleeping, 10

supplies, 4, 6–7, 9, 10, 12,
    15, 17
  aquariums, 4, 6, 9, 12, 17
  bowls, 7, 9, 12
  food, 7, 9, 10, 12
  sand, 7, 9, 12
  shells, 7, 17, 21
  water, 7, 15

temperature, 9

veterinarians, 15